Machines Inside Machines

Using Pulleys and Gears

Wendy Sadler

www.raintreepublishers.co.uk
Visit our website to find out more information about **Raintree** books.

To order:
☎ Phone 44 (0) 1865 888112
▤ Send a fax to 44 (0) 1865 314091
💻 Visit the Raintree Bookshop at **www.raintreepublishers.co.uk** to browse our catalogue and order online.

First published in Great Britain by Raintree,
Halley Court, Jordan Hill, Oxford, OX2 8EJ,
part of Harcourt Education.
Raintree is a registered trademark of Harcourt
Education Ltd.

Editorial: Melanie Copland and Kate Buckingham
Design: Michelle Lisseter, Victoria Bevan and
Bridge Creative Services Ltd
Picture Research: Hannah Taylor
Production: Duncan Gilbert

Originated by Repro Multi Warna
Printed and bound in China by South China
Printing Company

10 digit ISBN 1 844 43602 0 (hardback)
13 digit ISBN 978 1 844 43602 6 (hardback)
09 08 07 06 05
10 9 8 7 6 5 4 3 2 1

10 digit ISBN 1 844 43610 1 (paperback)
13 digit ISBN 978 1 844 43610 1 (paperback)
10 09 08 07 06
10 9 8 7 6 5 4 3 2 1

British Library Cataloguing in Publication Data
Sadler, Wendy
Using Pulleys and Gears. – (Machines
Inside Machines)
621.8'33
A full catalogue record for this book is available
from the British Library.

Acknowledgements
The publishers would like to thank the following
for permission to reproduce photographs:
Alamy Images (Leslie Garland Picture Library)
p. **11**; Alamy Images (Leslie Garland Picture
Library) pp. **13, 26**; Alamy Images (SCPhotos)
pp. **6, 14**; Corbis (Mark Hanauer) p. **5**; Corbis
(Sygma/Sandy Huffaker JR) p. **4**; Corbis (Craig
Aurness) p. **24**; Corbis (John & Lisa Merrill) p.
19; Corbis (Kevin Fleming) p. **9**; Corbis (Owen
Franken) p. **7**; Corbis (Ron Watts) p. **12**; Corbis
(Tim de Waele) p. **21**; DK Images p. **27**;
Harcourt Education Ltd (Trevor Clifford) pp. **16,
22**; Harcourt Education Ltd (Tudor Photography)
pp. **18, 20, 23, 25**; Peter Willis p. **29**; Powerstock
(age footstock) p. **15**.

Cover photograph of cogs reproduced with
permission of Getty Images/Taxi.

Every effort has been made to contact copyright
holders of any material reproduced in this book.
Any omissions will be rectified in subsequent
printings if notice is given to the publishers.

The paper used to print this book comes from
sustainable resources

Contents

Any words appearing in the text in bold,
like this, are explained in the glossary.

Pulleys are **simple machines**. A simple machine is something that helps us to do a job. Pulleys are made up of parts that include a wheel, an **axle**, and some rope. They are usually used to help people lift things up. You can find pulleys all around you.

Pulleys are being used on this boat to lower a whale back into the sea.

Gears are simple machines made up of a set of wheels with teeth around the edges. These wheels with teeth are called **cogs**. The cogs are linked together.

Gears are useful for changing the speed or direction of something that turns or spins. There are gears on bicycles and inside car **engines**. Different types of gear can make things move in different ways.

Gears on a bicycle help us to ride up steep hills.

Fixed pulleys

If you have curtains in your house they might use a pulley. When you want to open the curtains and see out of the window you pull down on the string. The pulley opens the curtains. This is a **fixed pulley**.

Have you used a pulley like this before?

A fixed pulley has a wheel that does not move from its position. It only turns round and round.

Flagpoles have fixed pulleys. The flag starts off at the bottom of the pole. When you pull downwards on the rope, the other end moves upwards. The flag is attached to this end so it also moves up the pole.

A fixed pulley changes the direction of the **force** you put in, but not the amount of force you need to do the job.

Moving pulleys

There are two types of pulley: a **fixed pulley** and a **moveable pulley**. A moveable pulley uses a wheel that is not fixed in one place, so it can move around along the rope. The moving part of the pulley is usually joined to the object you want to lift. The other end of the rope is fixed to something solid above the object you want to lift.

pull here

something solid

pulley wheel

heavy object

Moveable pulleys can help you to lift heavy objects you would not be able to lift on your own.

With a single moveable pulley you have to use your **effort force** to pull in the same direction as the object you want to lift. You need to pull the rope over a longer distance, but you need less effort force to lift the weight.

Climbers sometimes use moveable pulleys to rescue people if they have fallen. A moveable pulley is attached to a rope on their belt. The other end is attached to another climber who also has a pulley on their belt. If one climber falls, the other climber can use the moveable pulley to help pull them back to safety.

The moveable pulley on the stretcher helps the rescue team pull the wounded climber up.

9

Combined pulleys

A **combined pulley** has at least two wheels that turn as you pull on a rope. This is the most useful way to use pulleys.

Combined pulleys usually have one **fixed pulley** at the top, which is joined to something solid. There is usually one **moveable pulley**, which is joined on to the object that you are trying to lift. The fixed pulley changes the direction of the **force** you put in. The moveable pulley increases your force so you can lift heavy weights.

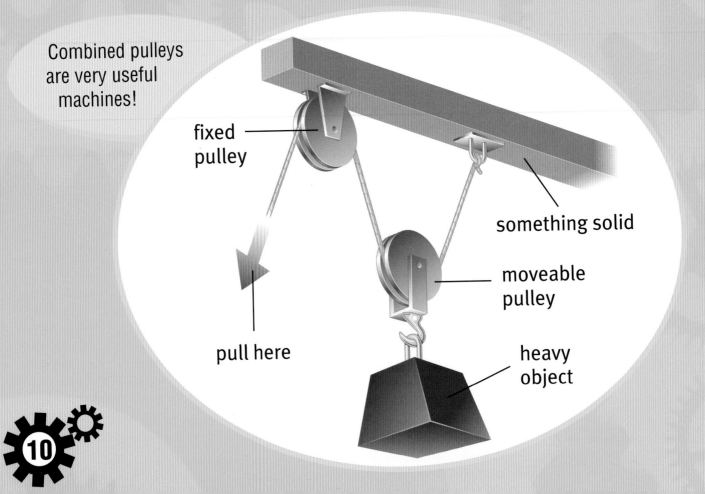

Combined pulleys are very useful machines!

fixed pulley

something solid

moveable pulley

pull here

heavy object

A pulley gives you something called a **mechanical advantage**. Mechanical advantage happens when you get more force out of a machine than you put into it. This means it reduces the **effort force** you need to lift something.

A combined pulley with two wheels needs half the effort force that you would need to lift something without a pulley. This means you can lift twice as much with your effort force when you use a pulley.

Pulleys are helping this man to lift his boat out of the water.

How much do pulleys help us?

People can use pulleys to help them clean very tall buildings. They sit on seats with ropes attached to them and to the top of the building. The ropes go around a **combined pulley**. Electric **motors** help pull the ropes that move the seats up and down. By using pulleys, the motor does not have to pull all the weight of each seat. It can pull with much less **force**, but it has to pull the ropes a long way.

This man is using a pulley to help him clean the windows of a very tall building.

Cranes

Cranes can lift very heavy objects such as cars, lorries, and big bricks for building houses. They use lots of pulleys to help reduce the amount of force needed.

A crane has lots of combined pulleys working together. Motors wind up the rope. Because the weights they lift are very heavy, the motors have to wind the rope a long way.

Cranes use pulleys to help lift very heavy weights such as these building blocks.

What would happen without...?

We need cranes to help us build tall buildings. Without cranes, all our buildings would probably be less than four floors high.

People and pulleys

At the gym, some people use machines with pulleys to lift weights. The machines exercise different parts of the body. Pulleys are used to change the direction of **force** that you need to lift the weights. For example, you might push downwards to lift a weight upwards. This means that they usually use a **fixed pulley**.

This machine has a handle that people pull down on to exercise.

In some countries people have to fetch water from a well. The water is quite deep down under the ground. It would be hard to reach without a rope. A bucket of water is heavy to lift so a fixed pulley at the top of the well makes it easier. The person needs less force to lift the water, and they can use the weight of their bodies to help them pull.

A pulley on a well helps to lift heavy buckets of water out of the ground.

What is a gear?

A gear is made up of two or more **cogs**. A cog is a wheel that has teeth around the edge. The teeth in the cogs fit together. When the first cog turns, the teeth push against the teeth in the second cog. This makes the second cog turn in the opposite direction. If we add a third cog then it turns in the same direction as the first cog.

first cog

If you turn the first cog, how many of the other cogs in this photograph will turn?

The cogs inside gears are not always right next to each other. Cogs can be joined together by belts or chains.

top cog

belt

chain

bottom cog

An escalator is a machine that you use instead of stairs. It uses gears. A **motor** turns the top cog. A belt joins the top cog to the bottom cog. This means that one motor can turn two cogs. When cogs are joined with a belt or chain they turn in the same direction.

How do we use gears?

We can use gears to change the speed of something that turns. To do this we need different sized **cogs** working together.

Cogs work together to control the speed of this toy car.

Activity

Fast to slow...
1. Find a plastic cog with 24 teeth and a smaller one, with 12 teeth.
2. Join the cogs by locking the teeth.
3. Turn the small cog round through one circle. The small cog has moved 12 teeth, and so has the large cog. The large cog is moving more slowly, so it has only moved half a circle.

Slow to fast...
1. Now turn the large cog in one circle. What happens?

A windmill is a machine that uses gears to **grind** up grain into flour. The wind blows the sails round. This makes a large cog turn. This cog is joined to a smaller cog. The small cog is joined to stones called millstones. The millstones grind the grain. They turn quickly because they are joined to the small cog.

This windmill uses gears to help it grind up grain.

sails

Bicycle gears

On a bicycle, gears of different sizes are fixed together. The gear **cog** by the pedal and the back wheel gear cogs are linked together by a chain. This fits over the teeth of the cogs. The chain always stays around the front gear cog, but it can move between the different sized back gear cogs.

When you change gear, the chain lifts off one gear cog and on to another.

The front cog, which drives the cogs, is joined to the pedals. You make the front gear turn by pushing the pedals with your feet.

20

When you are getting started on a bicycle, or trying to ride up a hill, the wheels of the bicycle need a large **force** to turn them. To help us we need the pedals to move the largest gear cog at the back. This means that the bicycle wheels turn at a low speed, but with a large force. You then need less force to push on the pedals.

In a high gear, the chain moves to a smaller gear wheel so you can go faster!

Groovy gears

Special gears called **worm gears** can be used to change the direction and speed of a turn. A worm gear has a rod with a screw shape on it, and a **cog** with teeth that fit into the spaces in the screw.

Worm gears are useful because they can slow down movement. When you turn the cog quickly, the rod with the screw moves much slower.

When you turn the cog, the teeth push against the spaces in the screw and make it turn slowly.

screw

cog

Another type of gear is called a **rack and pinion**. This gear can turn round and round movement into backwards and forwards movement.

A rack and pinion is made up of a cog and a straight piece of metal with teeth in it. When the cog turns, the teeth push against the teeth of the piece of metal. It moves forwards or backwards.

Some car window winders use a rack and pinion gear. The handle turns round and the window moves up and down.

Gears in the house and garden

A lawn sprinkler is a machine that uses lots of gears. The water flows into the sprinkler and turns a wheel called a turbine. The water then pushes out through holes in the top of the sprinkler.

The turbine spins very fast, so there are some **worm gears** inside that slow down the movement. The slow movement then drives a **crank**. The crank changes the turning movement into a side-to-side movement, so that the water reaches a large part of your garden.

Lots of **simple machines** are working together inside a lawn sprinkler.

Some egg whisks use gears. A handle is joined to a large **cog**. The large cog is connected with teeth to two smaller cogs. When the large cog turns it makes the small cogs turn quickly.

Activity

1. Ask an adult if they have an egg whisk like the one in this picture.
2. Turn the handle so that you do just one whole circle with the large cog. As you do this, see if you can count how many times the ends of the whisk turn round.

All cars have gears to make the car wheels turn at different speeds. A car also needs a gear **cog** that will make the wheels turn – so the car can turn corners. The drive shaft is a rod that joins the gearbox to the wheels of the car. In a low gear the car wheels turn quite slowly and in a high gear they turn very fast.

Can you see how many different cogs there are inside this gearbox?

There are many other gears inside a car. In some cars, the speedometer measures how fast the car is going. It also counts how many miles or kilometres the car has travelled since it was made.

Gears can be used to show how far a car has travelled.

The dials that show how far the car has travelled are connected to the wheels of the car. As the car moves, the car wheels turn. As the car wheels turn, the dials turn. The dials need to turn much more slowly than the car wheels, so a **worm gear** is used to slow them down.

The clockwork radio

The clockwork radio was **invented** in 1994. It uses lots of **simple machines** inside it.

1. Handle – you turn the handle to wind up the metal spring. When you stop winding, the spring wants to return to the shape it was before.

2. Spring – the spring unwinds slowly and turns the **axle** in the middle of the spring.

The clockwork radio is a **compound machine**.

88.2

3. Gears – the gears are used to turn the slow movement into fast movement that can make electricity. As the fast gear **cog** turns it makes electricity so the radio can work.

A clockwork radio
doesn't need electricity
to make it work. You give it
power by winding it up.

The clockwork radio is very important for people in places where there is no electricity supply. A radio helps people to learn about what is happening in the world and gives them important information.

All sorts of machines use pulleys and gears to do lots of different things. Have a look around your house and see how many you can find!

You can find out about **simple machines** by talking to your teacher or parents. Think about the simple machines you use every day – how do you think they work? Your local library will have books and information about this. You will find the answers to many of your questions in this book, but you can also use other books and the Internet.

Books to read

Science Around Us: Using Machines, Sally Hewitt (Chrysalis Children's Books, 2004)

Very Useful Machines: Pulleys, Chris Oxlade (Heinemann Library, 2003)

What do Pulleys and Gears do? David Glover (Heinemann Library, 2001)

Using the Internet

Explore the Internet to find out more about pulleys and gears. Try using a search engine such as www.yahooligans.com or www.internet4kids.com, and type in keywords such as 'pulley', 'gear', and **'worm gear'**.

Glossary

axle rod that goes through the centre of a wheel or group of wheels

cog wheel with teeth around the edge

combined pulley pulley made up of a fixed pulley and a moveable pulley working together

compound machine machine that uses two or more simple machines

crank part of a machine that changes round and round movement to side-to-side movement

effort force force that you put into a pulley or gear

engine machine that can make things move

fixed pulley pulley that changes the direction of the pull you put into it

force push or pull. Forces can make things move.

grind bash up into little pieces

invent to discover or make something for the first time

mechanical advantage when a machine is used to turn a small force into a larger force

motor machine that can make things move. Motors usually work using electricity.

moveable pulley pulley that makes the pull you put into it bigger – so you can lift heavy objects

rack and pinion gear that changes round and round movement into backwards and forwards movement

simple machine something that can change the effort force needed to move something, or change the direction it moves in

worm gear screw and cog working together

Index